Dear Ruth,

Thank you
very much

[signature]

The Magic of Chef Aldo

His
"True Taste of ITALY"
Favorites

Table of Contents

Publication Information

ISBN 0-9629299-1-3
Printed in USA
Published by Andiamo Italia
7096 14 Mile Road
Warren, Michigan 48092

Photography by Kurt Taylor
Written by Aldo Ottaviani, Tom Vitale and Larry Fanale

To Joanne -

*Whose love and support
meant so much to my life.*

Forward

Years ago we went to St. Louis for the Stanley Cup playoffs. Ah, I thought, now we'd get some real Italian food. We'd go to The Hill, the celebrated section where Yogi Berra and Joe Garagiola grew up, and we'd dine on the real thing.

Six of us writers went out to dinner one night, and I took them to The Hill. We went to one of the old established restaurants but my heart sank when I looked at the menu. No spaghetti with meat sauce.

It had happened again. They were serving green noodles, orange noodles, even red noodles, and you could get them with broccoli, brussels sprouts and, I swear, even fish eyes.

I said to the owner: "How come you don't have spaghetti with meat sauce on the menu?"

He replied: "We don't want those kind of people in here."

Guess who got up and left? The six of us went searching for a steak house.

Which brings me to my friend, Aldo Ottaviani, the man who wrote this cook book. How privileged I've been in my life. I've seen the greatest basketball player of all time, Michael Jordan. I've seen the greatest hockey player, Gordie Howe. I've seen the greatest golfer, Jack Nicklaus. And now I have seen the greatest chef, Mr. Aldo.

Let me put it this way: Do you take the seeds out of the tomatoes when you make spaghetti sauce? That's the secret. Aldo taught it to my wife. It may sound simple, and even a little stupid, but try it. There is acid in those seeds and they can make the sauce bitter. Just cut the tomatoes in half, hold them under some running water, and they come out very easily.

The result is the sweetest, tastiest sauce this side of heaven. Or, at least, this side of Bari, Italy, where my man was born and learned to cook.

I know Rembrandt cannot teach us to paint, but this man can come close. Yes, he's a fuss-budget over how to do things. He never takes the easy way. When he ran his own restaurant - Aldo's at Moross and Kelly for nearly 40 years - he got up at 7a.m. and went to the market to buy the freshest food stuffs for that day's menu. He'd bake his own bread, make his own soup - even cure his own prosciutto. And, he would cut his veal as it was needed for each order.

My wife and I would go to his restaurant twice a week (100 mile round trip from Clarkston) and the finest moments of our lives were those Sunday afternoons, when all my work was done and the winter sun was setting in the cold, darkening skies, and we were just pulling into the parking lot next to Aldo's. We knew that for the next three or four hours not only would we be treated to the finest cooking in Detroit, but there would be Mrs. Aldo and Maria who handled the pasta, and Donna, the waitress, to warm the evening with their caring ways.

When Mrs. Aldo (our beloved Joanne) passed away several years ago, I thought Mr. Aldo would be finished. He loved her as no man ever loved his wife. He needed her. She meant everything to him. And when she was gone, I feared for my man. He is such a kind and gentle person but he has never been caught up in the world around him. Almost his entire existence is in the kitchen and when that was taken from him . . . well, my wife and I prayed for him.

Along came Joe Vicari, Aldo's old friend - the man who owns Andiamo's Restaurant - and Joe asked Aldo if he would help him with his new restaurant. Would he show the younger chefs a few things in the kitchen, and darned if they didn't listen. These chefs - superb cooks in their own right - have brought Aldo back to life and given our community the kind of Italian food that is simply pleasurable to everyone.

And let's not forget the third member of this trio of friends. the late Angelo Veneri, who goes way back in this town - a long-time friend of Aldo, Joe and myself, and no kinder many ever lived. He was the man inside the door at Andiamo's, the one who made you feel welcome with that warm smile and handshake which was so sincere because it came from his heart. (Angelo may have been my favorite because he would slip us a couple of quarts of meat sauce when we were leaving.)

If all this sounds like a paid political announcement, so be it. I'll just have a plate of spaghetti and heavy on the meat sauce, please.

Joe Falls, Sports Editor, Detroit News

About the man we know and love

If the care and preparation of Italian food is an art, Aldo Ottaviani is truly a master. "Mr. Aldo," as he is lovingly known, is the Master Chef at Andiamo Italia, the very popular and successful restaurant in Warren, Michigan. On May 3rd, 1948, while his wife to be, Joanne was visiting Rome as a tourist, the two meet. By the 1st of June, they were married. Together, they came to the United States and settled in Detroit, Michigan. Mr. Aldo spoke no English, his wife helped him interpret the language of this new land.

In 1950, Mr. Aldo and Joanne opened "Aldo's" restaurant. Initially pizza was the bill-of-fare. With $2,500 borrowed, they operated for almost 40 years, one of the most successful and highly regarded Italian restaurants in the metropolitan Detroit area. Still working as his interpreter, Joanne worked with him day and night, greeting customers, working the cash register and helping him buy the necessities for the restaurant. After many years of hard work, Mr. Aldo decided to retire. Soon after, Joe Vicari, who operates Andiamo Italia, offered Mr. Aldo full reign as Master Chef. They now share a mutual admiration that today is both personal and professional.

To know Mr. Aldo is to understand that he is a man without compromise. Fresh ingredients and meticulous care are essential to the preparation of his wonderful dishes. Mr. Aldo describes it as "love..., a lot of love!! Every day I think, what can I do to improve and be successful with the food I prepare for my customers." Italian cooking is many times misunderstood, over-spiced and harsh. Not so with Mr. Aldo. His philosophy on cooking is simple. "Your food should be digestible, and it should be nutritious." Nutrition plays a very important role in the way he prepares his recipes. Only the freshest of ingredients and quality cuts of meat, fish and poultry go into the dishes he prepares. This philosophy comes from his many years of experience here in America. "We are blessed because we can find all the fine herbs and best ingredients that sometimes can't be found elsewhere in the world," says Mr. Aldo.

He has been kind enough to share his recipes and procedures to all who wish to enjoy a variety of his delightful Italian dishes in their own home. Discover the flavors that are ever so subtle and distinctive by the man who has brought dining enjoyment to so many people for almost half of a century. From antipasto to dessert, chef Aldo's love affair with wholesome delightful cooking can now be yours to enjoy.

Along with the following recipes, Mr. Aldo also offers some simple but very helpful hints to the successful culinary preparation of of all kinds.

- Follow the procedures as they are described. The recipes will turn out exactly the way you'll expect them to be.

- Wash all fresh vegetables and fruit thoroughly. This will rid them of any commercial sprays or pesticides.

- When choosing fresh vegetables, always remember, they are best when bought in season.

- Tomato sauces are done and at their peak of flavor when the oil comes to the top.

- For the recipes in this book vegetables should be thoroughly cooked.

- Finally, be it vegetables, fruit, meat, poultry or fish, organic products not only produce better flavor but are also more nutritious.

Bon Appetite!

Antipasti

Calamari in Umido Con Piselli

Calamari in Light Tomato Sauce and Peas

Ingredients / Serves 6

2 1/2 lbs sliced calamari	1 teaspoon lemon juice
1 cup peas	2 oz tomato paste
1 cup water	1 teaspoon basil
1 pinch salt	1 tablespoon Italian parsley, chopped
1 pinch sugar	
Olive oil	Salt and pepper to taste
1/2 Spanish onion, diced	

To clean calamari wash thoroughly, remove skin, head and bones from the body. Squeeze the remainder of the insides from body. Re-wash body and legs. Slice calamari in rings.

For peas:

In a sauce pan put peas and 1 cup of water with 1 pinch of salt and 1 pinch of sugar. Bring to a boil and cook 5-6 minutes. Remove from stove and keep peas in water until added to calamari. This procedure will retain the color of the peas.

Coat saute pan with olive oil, add calamari and diced onion with a dash of salt. Saute calamari until it changes to a reddish color and onions become tender. Add lemon juice, tomato paste, drained peas, basil, parsley and some water to dilute tomato paste. Cook for approximately 10 minutes or until done. Salt and pepper to taste and serve.

Note:

If using fresh peas, start with boiling water, if using frozen peas start with cold water.

A tasty approach for calamari lovers.

Code Di Aragosta in Salsa Picante

Lobster in a Lemon Piquant Sauce

Ingredients / Serves 6

6 - 8 oz cold water lobster tails

1/2 onion, sliced

1 oz red wine vinegar

2 stalks celery, sliced on the bias

1 carrot, sliced

10 black pepper corns

Olive oil

1 leek, sliced thin

3 oz white wine

Juice of 1/2 lemon

1 teaspoon Dijon mustard

1 tablespoon flour

2 tablespoons water

1/2 teaspoon tomato paste

18 green olives, pitted

1 pinch parsley

Boil lobster tails in cold water, with onion, vinegar, celery, carrot and black pepper corns. Cook until lobster is done, approximately 6-8 minutes. Remove from water, split shell down the back and remove lobster meat. Discard vegetables.

Coat saute pan with olive oil, add lobster tails and saute for 5 minutes, then add leeks to lobster pan.

Mix together wine, lemon juice, Dijon mustard then add to lobster. Next sprinkle with flour, and cook until wine reduces. Add water, tomato paste, green olives and parsley.

Reduce to desired consistency and serve.

Aldo's contribution to an elegant appetizer.

Melanzane Grigliate Ai Gamberi

Grilled Eggplant topped with Fresh Water Shrimp

Ingredients / Serves 6

6 slices of eggplant, cut lengthwise approximately 1/2" thick

Salt

Olive oil

Pepper

18 medium shrimp, peeled and deveined

1 leek, sliced thin

1 teaspoon flour

1 tablespoon fresh parsley, chopped

1 teaspoon dry basil

1 tablespoon tomato paste

Juice of 1/2 lemon

1 pinch dry mustard

2 tablespoons whipping cream

1/2 lb mozzarella cheese, shredded

Sprinkle eggplant with salt. Layer salted eggplant in strainer and cover with a weighted object. (This procedure allows bitter water from the eggplant to drain as it sits.) Set aside for 40 minutes. Rinse salt off and pat dry with paper towel.

Brush eggplant with olive oil and place in broiler or on grill, season with pepper and place in baking pan.

Coat saute pan with olive oil, add shrimp and sliced leek, saute until water from shrimp is absorbed. Sprinkle shrimp with flour. Add parsley, basil, tomato paste, lemon juice and dry mustard, cook 5 to 8 minutes. Toward the end of cooking add whipping cream.

Divide shrimp mixture evenly over eggplant, sprinkle with shredded mozzarella cheese and bake in preheated oven at 350° F until cheese is melted and serve.

A tasty combination of shrimp and eggplant.

Funghi Portabello Ripieni Alla Aldo

Portabello Mushrooms stuffed with Crab Meat Aldo

Ingredients / Serves 6

6 large Portabello mushrooms

1 pinch salt

Juice of 1/2 lemon

1 oz white wine

Extra virgin olive oil

2 garlic cloves, mashed

1/2 teaspoon anchovy paste

1/2 tablespoon parsley

1 pinch basil

1 pinch oregano

1 1/2 lbs Alaskan king crab meat, shredded

Salt and pepper to taste

2 slices of white bread, no crust

6 slices Fontina cheese

1 pinch Paprika

Start by cleaning mushrooms. Cut stems from caps (to be used for filling.) Cook in boiling water with a pinch of salt, lemon juice and white wine.

When water boils cook for 2 minutes, remove mushrooms and let cool.

For filling:

Finely chop mushroom stems.

In a saute pan warm olive oil and garlic. Cook until garlic is golden brown, then remove garlic.

Add chopped mushroom stems, anchovy paste, parsley, basil, oregano, crab meat, salt and pepper to taste. Add bread so mixture binds. Saute 4 to 5 minutes.

Stuff filling into each mushroom cap, top with Fontina cheese and sprinkle with paprika. Bake at 350° F in a preheated oven until cheese is melted and serve.

A rich and flavorful beginning to any meal.

Zuppe

Brodo Di Pollo Alla Giardinièra

Chicken Soup with Garden Vegetables

Ingredients / Serves 6

For broth:

1 - 5 lb whole chicken

Handful of salt

2 onions, chopped in 3 inch pieces

2 carrots, chopped in 3 inch pieces

2 celery stalks with tops, chopped in 3 inch pieces

1 bay leaf

6 black peppercorns

2 cloves

1 pinch of parsley

2 pear tomatoes, chopped

For soup:

2 onions, julienne cut

3 carrots cut round

3 celery stalks with tops, cut on the bias and chop tops

2 cups peas

3/4 cup pasta

Broth:

Start broth by placing whole chicken in a pot with cold water and a handful of salt.

Add to chicken, 2 onions, 2 carrots, 2 celery stalks, all chopped in 3 inch lengths. Add bay leaf, black peppercorns, cloves, parsley, and pear tomatoes.

Bring to a boil and simmer for 3 hours. As water reduces, replenish with same amount until chicken is done.

Remove chicken from broth. Set aside.

Strain broth through a very fine strainer and discard all waste. Refrigerate broth overnight.

Soup:

Next day, remove grease from top of broth. Add 2 onions julienne, 3 carrots cut round, 3 celery stalks cut on the bias with chopped tops, and 2 cups of peas.

Bring broth and vegetables to a boil, reduce heat and let simmer until vegetables are tender. Approximately 45 minutes. Add pasta and continue for an additional 10 minutes.

Fresh seasonal vegetables will enhance the flavor of this delightful soup.

Crema Di Verdure Di Stagione

Cream Vegetable Soup of the Season

Ingredients / Serves 6

1 head cauliflower	5 tablespoons flour
1 bunch broccoli	6 cups chicken broth, warmed
1 pinch salt	
1 onion, chopped fine	2 cups milk, warm
3 celery stalks with tops, chopped fine	1 pinch fresh parsley, chopped
	1 pinch Basil
3 carrots, chopped fine	Salt
6 tablespoons butter	White pepper

Clean cauliflower and broccoli thoroughly saving the leaves.

Boil the broccoli, cauliflower and leaves with a pinch of salt until tender and drain. Set aside half of the cauliflower buds to add later.

Chop onion and celery fine and set aside. Place leaves and the remainder of the cauliflower buds and carrots in a food processor until very fine and set aside.

In a soup pot melt butter and saute chopped onions and celery. Cook to a golden color.

When ingredients are tender remove from heat, add flour and mix throughly. For desired consistancy return to heat and cook 1 minute.

Add warm broth and bring to a boil. Add processed cauliflower, carrots and leaves, let simmer.

Add warm milk, parsley, basil, adjust seasonings, add remaining cauliflower and broccoli. Cook for 10 minutes and serve.

Other seasonal vegetables may be used, such as tomato or asparagus.

21

Minestrone Alla Aldo

Aldo's own Minestrone

Ingredients / Serves 6

2 cups Cranberry beans, precooked	1 head of Romaine lettuce, chopped
Water to cover beans	3 ripe tomatoes, diced
3 cloves garlic, mashed	1 tablespoon tomato paste
1/4 teaspoon sage	6 tablespoons olive oil
1 large Spanish onion, diced	1 pinch marjoram
2 carrots diced fine	1 pinch basil
2 celery stalks, diced fine	1 tablespoon parsley
2 medium potatoes, diced 1/2"	1 pinch rosemary
2 small turnips, diced 1/2"	Salt and pepper to taste
1/4 head of Savory cabbage, chopped	

Begin by soaking beans overnight in cold water.

Cook beans with same water they soaked in, with mashed garlic and sage. When beans are done turn off and set aside for approximately 45 minutes. Save water to add later.

In a soup pot place all the vegetables and enough cold water to cover vegetables, bring to a boil. Let simmer until tender and add tomato paste and olive oil.

Next, add beans, with additional water and add marjoram, basil, parsley, rosemary, salt and pepper to taste. Let simmer for another 10 minutes and serve.

This is the best of a true Italian soup classic.

Pasta & Fagioli Del Contadino

Pasta and Bean Soup Farmer Style

Ingredients / Serves 6

1 1/2 lbs Canellini beans

2 pinches rosemary

2 pinches sage

3 cloves

2 cloves garlic, mashed

6 tablespoons olive oil

4 oz ground panchetta (optional)

3 celery stalks, diced fine

1 onion, diced fine

2 carrots, diced fine

2 pinches parsley, chopped

2 tablespoons tomato paste

Salt and pepper to taste

Cover beans with water. Add 1 pinch rosemary, 1 pinch sage, cloves and 3 cloves mashed garlic. Bring to a boil and cook approximately 20 minutes. At this point discard water. Add fresh hot water to beans and return to boil and let simmer until tender. Set aside and leave in water.

(Puree) 1/4 of the beans with some of the water they were cooked in to make a fine paste.

Cover bottom of a soup pot with olive oil and heat. Add ground panchetta and cook until brown.

Add celery, onions, and carrots, and cook until tender.

Add 2 pinches parsley, 1 pinch rosemary, 1 pinch sage, whole beans, bean puree, tomato paste and the remainder of water the beans were cooked in.

Add additional water if soup is too thick and simmer.

Add salt and pepper to taste. Serve with desired pasta.

A simple rendition of an old country favorite.

Insalate

Insalata Mista La Capricciosa

Mixed Green Salad

Ingredients / serves 6

1/2 head Iceberg lettuce

4 leaves of red leaf lettuce

1 head of Boston lettuce

4 leaves Romaine lettuce

1 Belgium endive, julienne sliced

3 Beefsteak tomatoes, sliced

1 seedless cucumber, sliced thin

3/4 lb Feta cheese

18 black olives, pitted

Dressing

1/4 cup extra virgin olive oil

2 tablespoons red wine vinegar

2 cloves garlic, crushed

Salt and pepper to taste

Tear lettuce by hand and wash. Slice endive, tomatoes and cucumbers. Cut Feta cheese into 1/2 inch cubes.

Dressing:

In mixing bowl combine olive oil, vinegar, crushed garlic and salt and pepper to taste. Beat by hand for smooth consistency.

Toss with lettuce, cucumber, tomatoes, olives and cheese, serve cold.

The inclusion of the Feta cheese brings a delightful flavor accent to this salad.

Insalata Di' Estate Ai Gamberi

Summer Time Salad with Shrimp

Ingredients / Serves 6

12 baby artichokes

1/2 cup white wine

1 tablespoon flour

2 cups water

30 shrimp (21-25 count)

1 carrot, chopped

1 celery stalk, chopped

1 onion, sliced

Juice from 2 fresh lemons

1 cup olive oil

1 tablespoons Italian parsley, chopped

12 leaves red leaf lettuce

Salt

Black pepper corns

Clean baby artichokes by skinning the stem and removing the outer leaves until white leaves appear. Boil water with a pinch of salt.

In small mixing bowl combine wine and flour. Add cleaned artichokes, wine and flour mixture to 2 cups boiling water. Cook until tops of artichokes are tender, test with toothpick. Remove from water and cool.

In boiling water cook shrimp in shells along with 1 chopped carrot, 1 chopped celery stalk, and 1 sliced onion. When water boils a second time cook approximately 2 minutes. Cool shrimp in cold water, finally remove shells, devein and cut in half.

In second mixing bowl combine lemon juice, olive oil, and parsley. Add cooled shrimp and artichokes to mixture and let marinate for 15 minutes.

Place 2 leaves of red leaf lettuce on each salad plate and add artichokes and shrimp divided equally.

Salt and pepper corns to taste, and serve.

An elegant dish in both taste and visual presentation.

Insalata Rustica Di Fagioli Alla Toscana

Cannelini Bean Salad

Ingredients / Serves 6

2 lbs of dry Cannelini beans

Water to boil beans

2 cloves garlic, mashed

3 cloves

1/2 teaspoon sage

1 Spanish onion, soaked in water to remove acids, sliced

1/4 cup wine vinegar (optional)

2/3 cup olive oil

2 tablespoons Italian parsley, chopped

Salt and pepper to taste

1 head Radicchio lettuce, julienne

Soak Cannelini beans overnight in water.

The following day boil beans, in same water with two cloves of mashed garlic, 3 cloves, water and 1/2 teaspoon sage. When beans are soft add salt then drain water and discard garlic. Place in bowl.

Toss beans with sliced onions and wine vinegar, olive oil, parsley and add salt and pepper to taste.

Place julienne Radicchio lettuce on plates and top with bean salad mixture.

This salad takes on a wonderful blend of flavors. You may want to add Beefsteak tomatoes for garnish.

Insalate Primavera

Spring Time Salad

Ingredients / Serves 6

1 pound fresh green beans	Salt
2 seedless cucumbers, sliced on the bias	Fresh ground pepper
	1 cup olive oil
1 medium size sweet red onion, sliced	1 pinch parsley
1/3 cup red wine vinegar	6 hard boiled eggs, wedged

Add beans to boiling water with a pinch of salt and cook until tender, drain and set aside. Place beans in a bowl and add salt and pepper to taste.

Peel and slice cucumbers, set aside. Place onion in cold water for 20 minutes, to remove acids. Remove and slice very thin.

Dressing:

In mixing bowl combine vinegar, salt and pepper to taste. Add olive oil and parsley, beat by hand.

Divide beans onto 6 salad plates in center of plates. Arrange eggs and sliced cucumbers around the beans. Place sliced red onion on top of beans and finish by topping with dressing.

A classic Italian salad with Mr. Aldo's special touch.

Pasta & Salsa

Gnocchi

Potato Dumplings

Ingredients / Serves 6

3 Idaho potatoes (80 count)	2 egg yolks
1/2 stick of butter	4 cups Velvet cake flour
1 pinch salt	
2 tablespoons Parmesan cheese, grated	

Cook potatoes with skins in boiling water until tender. Drain and remove skins when potatoes reach room temperature. Mash potatoes with potato ricer until smooth. In a large bowl mix potatoes by hand with butter, salt, Parmesan cheese and egg yolks.

Slowly add Velvet cake flour to mixture and continue to knead dough until firm. When dough is firm, divide into 4 pieces and roll each into a long tube about 1/2 inch thick. Cut each tube in 1/2 inch pieces. Score each Gnocchi by using a fork to make a line then shape.

Boil in salted water until Gnocchi rise to the top, strain and serve.

Note:

You might need more or less flour depending on water content of the potatoes. Be careful not to add too much.

These dumplings will go well with Bolognese Alla Aldo.

Homemade Pasta Dough

Ingredients / Serves 6

1 1/4 lbs all purpose flour   6 whole eggs

1 teaspoon salt   1 teaspoon olive oil

For ravioli, canelloni, manicotti and lasagna dough add 1 tablespoon water for proper consistency

Pour flour into mixing bowl, make a hole in the center, add salt, eggs and olive oil. Slowly mix by hand, continue by kneading the dough until firm. Let dough rest for 20 minutes prior to rolling.

Roll dough to desired thickness. Cut by hand or use a manual pasta machine to roll and cut the shape of noodle you desire. Boil salted water and cook pasta to desired consistency and serve.

Note: if dough is too thick, add a small amount of water and knead again.

Nothing can substitute the flavor and texture of fresh homemade pasta.

Salsa Con Filetto Di Pollo Alla Aldo

Tomato Sauce with Chicken Tenderloin Aldo Style

Ingredients / Serves 6

8 oz mushrooms, sliced and poached

1 lemon wedge

1/4 cup white wine

Olive oil

2 garlic cloves, whole

6 chicken filets, diced

1/4 cup flour

4 oz ground panchetta

1/2 celery stalk, diced fine

1 carrot, diced fine

1 onion, diced fine

1 Hungarian pepper, diced fine

1 pinch sage

1 pinch rosemary

1 pinch basil

1 teaspoon parsley

2 oz dry sherry

2 oz butter

16 oz tomatoes, crushed

6 teaspoons tomato paste

1 1/2 cup water

Salt and pepper to taste

To poach mushrooms, boil water with lemon wedge, salt, and 1/4 cup white wine. Add mushrooms and boil for 8 minutes. Drain, pat dry and set aside.

Heat a large sauce pan, coat bottom of pan with olive oil and add garlic. Remove garlic when golden brown. Dust chicken lightly with flour. Add chicken and panchetta to pan and cook until brown. Season chicken with salt and pepper.

Add celery, carrot, onions, Hungarian pepper, mushrooms, sage, rosemary, basil, parsley, and salt and pepper to taste. Stir ingredients. Add sherry and cook until completely absorbed. Add butter, tomatoes, tomato paste, water and continue cooking for 45 minutes and serve.

Chicken brings a distinctive flavor to this sauce.

Fettucine Al Burro & Parmagiano

Fettucine with Butter and Cheese

Ingredients / Serves 6

1 lb homemade fettucine	3 oz Parmesan cheese, grated
4 oz unsalted butter	1/4 cup heavy cream
4 oz Mascarpone cheese	Salt and pepper to taste

Cook fettucine first. In saute pan add butter and Mascarpone cheese. When fettucine is cooked, add to pan and add a little water on the noodles then place pan on burner. Mix noodles with butter and mascarpone cheese then add Parmesan cheese and whipping cream and stir continuously. Last add salt and pepper to taste.

Note: All pasta should be cooked in salted water.

This sauce is Aldo's version of a classic Fettucine with Butter and Cheese.

Bolognese Alla Aldo

Meat Sauce Alla Aldo

Ingredients / Serves 6

1 Spanish onion

2 celery stalks

2 carrots

1/4 bunch fresh parsley

1 1/2 tablespoons dry basil

2 cloves garlic

1/8 lb panchetta

1 1/2 cup extra virgin olive oil

1/2 lb ground veal

1/2 lb ground pork

1/2 lb ground beef

1/2 teaspoon marjoram

1 pinch thyme

3 tablespoons salt

2 pinches pepper

1/4 cup burgundy wine

6 tablespoons tomato paste

2 - 32 oz cans pear tomatoes, peeled, seeded and chopped

3 cups water

1/2 cup heavy whipping cream

1 teaspoon sugar (optional)

Begin by grinding in a food processor or blender, onions, celery, carrots, parsley, basil, garlic and panchetta. Heat a large sauce pan with olive oil and cook the above mixture until hot.

Add veal, pork, beef, marjoram, thyme, 1 tablespoon salt, 1 pinch pepper and cook until brown. Add burgundy wine and cook until wine is completely absorbed. Add tomato paste, chopped tomatoes, water, 2 tablespoons salt, 1 pinch pepper, and let simmer until hot.

In a saute pan heat whipping cream, add to the tomato sauce and mix thoroughly. Note, sugar may be added if sauce is too tart. Simmer until the oil rises to the top. Remove excess oil and serve.

A sauce with a light Northern Italian accent.

Salsa Al Pomadoro Alla Toscana

Tomato Sauce with Herbs and Vegetables

Ingredients / Serves 6

1 Spanish onion	4 tablespoons tomato paste
3 celery stalks, with leaves	3 cups water
3 carrots	8 fresh basil leaves, chopped
1/4 bunch fresh parsley	1 pinch thyme
2 cloves garlic	1 pinch marjoram
1 1/2 cups extra virgin olive oil	1/2 cup milk
2-32 oz cans pear tomatoes, seeded and ground	Salt and pepper to taste

Grind onion, celery, carrots, parsley and garlic in a food processor or blender. In a large sauce pan coated with olive oil, cook until ingredients turn golden brown.

Add ground tomatoes, tomato paste, water, basil, thyme, marjoram, salt and pepper to taste. Let simmer approximately 1 hour. Add warm milk. Simmer again until the oil rises to the top. Skim off excess oil and serve.

A hearty tomato sauce that goes with a variety of pastas.

Salsa Tutto Mare

Sauce with Seafood

Ingredients / Serves 6

1/2 cup olive oil

2 cloves garlic

1 Spanish onion, chopped

6 pieces calamari, cleaned and sliced

6 shrimp (16-20 count), peeled and deveined

3 sea scallops, cut in half

1/2 tablespoon fresh oregano

1 tablespoon fresh basil, chopped

2 tablespoons parsley, chopped

1 pinch crushed red pepper seeds

4 tablespoons tomato paste

1 cup water

12 canned pear tomatoes, seeded and chopped

Salt and pepper to taste

In a large sauce pan heat olive oil and garlic. Remove garlic when golden brown. Add onions and calamari. Cook until tender.

Add shrimp, sea scallops, and cook for 8 minutes.

Add oregano, basil, parsley, red pepper seeds, salt and pepper to taste, tomato paste, water, pear tomatoes, and cook approximately 45 minutes to 1 hour for medium consistency and serve.

This recipe is Aldo's own Fruit of the Sea.

Manzo

Bistecca Di Lombo Alla Siciliana

New York Strip Steak Sicilian Style

Ingredients / Serves 6

6 - 8 oz New York Strip Steaks

Olive oil

Bread crumbs

2 medium onions, julienne

12 fresh Roma tomatoes, peeled, seeded

2 tablespoons fresh parsley, chopped

1 tablespoon fresh basil

1/2 teaspoon oregano

30 black olives, pitted

Salt and Pepper to taste

Preheat oven to 450° F.

Coat a large shallow baking pan with olive oil. Add steaks coated with bread crumbs. Cook on stove top approximately 2 minutes each side on high heat. Remove the steaks and set aside. Add onions, tomatoes, parsley, basil, oregano, black olives, and a little water. Stir mixture thoroughly with a tablespoon until warm. Return steaks to pan. Add salt and pepper to taste.

Bake until desired wellness is achieved. Approximately 12 minutes for medium. Place on a serving platter. Remove excess oil from pan and pour remaining sauce over and serve.

A New York Strip Steak that is seasoned to perfection.

Braciole Di Manzo Alla Aldo

Sliced Sirloin (Top Butt) with Raisins, Seasoned Pork, and Pine Nuts

Ingredients / Serves 6

12 oz ground pork

2/3 cup white raisins, soaked in water for 1/2 hour and drained

1/2 teaspoon rosemary

1/4 cup pine nuts

1 whole egg

1 tablespoon parsley

6 - 4 oz slices of sirloin (top butt pounded thin)

Flour

Olive oil

3 cloves garlic

1/2 cup white wine

2 stalks celery, chopped

1 large Spanish onion, julienne

2 medium carrots, chopped

1/4 cup water

Salt and Pepper to taste

Preheat oven to 450° F.

For filling: In a large bowl mix thoroughly, ground pork, raisins, rosemary, pine nuts, egg, parsley, salt and pepper to taste. Set aside.

Pound beef thin, season one side with salt and pepper to taste. Spread filling over beef. Roll each piece and hold together with toothpicks. Dust with flour. Heat a large shallow baking pan on stove top with olive oil and garlic. Remove garlic when golden brown. Place beef rolls in pan and brown on all sides. Add wine, when wine is absorbed add celery, onions, carrots, salt and pepper to taste, cover meat with water then place pan in oven. Cover with aluminum foil and finish cooking until tender. Remove from oven and set beef rolls aside. Remove excess oil from pan, if sauce is too thin you may add flour, if sauce is too thick add a little water. Strain gravy, discard vegetables, pour over meat and serve.

This simple beef entree can be served with either a vegetable or pasta.

Bistecca Di Costa Di Manzo Alla Pizzaiola

Boneless Beef Rib Steak

Ingredients / Serves 6

6 - 1/2" thick cut boneless beef rib eye steaks

1/2 cup olive oil

6 cloves garlic, halved

Flour

6 Roma tomatoes, peeled and seeded

1 tablespoon fresh parsley, chopped

1 tablespoon fresh basil

1 pinch dry oregano

1/4 cup water

1 pinch sugar

Salt and pepper to taste

Preheat oven to 450° F.

Heat a saute pan with olive oil and garlic. Lightly dust rib steaks with flour, add to pan and cook approximately 2 minutes on each side. Remove steaks from pan, set aside.

Add tomatoes, parsley, basil, oregano, cold water and sugar. Stir thoroughly with a tablespoon until warm. Return steaks to pan. Add salt and pepper to taste and cook approximately 2 minutes. Place mixture into a large shallow baking pan. Bake until desired wellness of steak is achieved. Approximately 8 minutes for medium and serve.

A hearty Italian red wine is a perfect accompaniment.

Spezzato Di Filetto Di Manzo Con Funghi & Piselli

Tenderloin Tips Sauteed with Garlic, Onion, Mushrooms, Peas and Burgundy Wine

Ingredients / Serves 6

1 1/2 lbs mushrooms, sliced

2 lbs tenderloin tips, cubed

1/2 cup olive oil

3 cloves garlic, mashed

1 pinch rosemary

1 pinch thyme

1 tablespoon parsley

2 medium Spanish onions, julienne

1/4 cup burgundy wine

2 tablespoons flour

Water

3 cups peas

Salt and pepper to taste

Boil mushroom for 8 minutes, drain and set aside.

Coat a large saute pan with olive oil. Place meat in pan with mashed garlic. Brown meat on all sides. Add rosemary, thyme, parsley, onions, poached mushrooms and burgundy wine. Cook until wine is absorbed.

Sprinkle meat with flour then add water to pan to cover meat, and add peas. Cook over medium heat until tender. Add water if sauce is too thick, stirring thoroughly. Remove any excess oil and serve.

Served over fettucine is an excellent option.

Filetto Di Manzo Ripieno Alla Aldo

Beef Tenderloin Filets Stuffed with Prosciutto, and Fontina Cheese

Ingredients / Serves 6

6 - 7 oz choice beef tenderloin butterfly cut filets

6 slices Prosciutto ham

6 slices Fontina cheese

Flour

Olive oil

4 cloves garlic, whole

1 Pinch rosemary, for each filet

1 pinch thyme, for each filet

1/2 cup Madeira Wine

6 slices fresh tomatoes, 1/4 inch thick

Bread crumbs

1 Pinch parsley

2 Pinches fresh basil

Preheat oven to 450° F.

Butterfly filets. Lightly salt and pepper. Add 1 slice of Prosciutto and 1 slice of Fontina cheese to each. Fold together, pierce with toothpick. Lightly dust each filet with flour.

Coat a large shallow baking pan with olive oil. Add garlic. and heat. Remove garlic when golden brown. Place filets in pan. Sprinkle each with a pinch of rosemary and a pinch of thyme. Cook on both sides for 3 minutes on high heat. Add Madeira wine and cook until absorbed. Remove excess oil from pan. Place sliced Tomato on each filet, salt and pepper to taste. Sprinkle with bread crumbs, parsley and fresh basil. Place in oven.

Bake until desired wellness is achieved, 15 to 20 minutes for medium, and serve.

The flavor of the Prosciutto stands out in this tenderloin entree.

Animelle Di Vitello Alla Aldo

Sweet Breads Aldo Style

Ingredients / Serves 6

2 lbs sweet breads

5 cups water

1/4 cup vinegar

Olive oil

1/4 stick butter

4 shallots, sliced

Flour

1 tablespoon parsley

1 lb par boiled mushrooms, sliced

2 pinches basil

1/4 cup Chablis wine

4 drops fresh lemon juice

1/4 teaspoon mustard

Salt and pepper to taste

In a sauce pan add water and vinegar with sweet breads. Bring to a boil for 10 minutes. Drain and cool sweet breads with cold water. Remove skin from sweet breads, cover with a clean towel with a weight on top to flatten. Next, slice sweet breads approximately 1/2" thick and set aside.

Coat a saute pan with olive oil and add butter. When butter is melted, add sliced shallots and flour dusted sweet breads. Next, add parsley, sliced mushrooms, basil, salt and pepper to taste. Mix wine, lemon juice, and mustard, add to mixture. Finish cooking and serve.

A recipe that will surely please the sweet bread lover.

Vitello

Veal Saltimbocca Alla Romana

Sauteed Veal with Prosciutto Ham

Ingredients / Serves 4

8 - 3 oz slices of veal	1 teaspoon dry Marsala wine
Flour	4 tablespoons butter
Olive oil	3 tablespoons water
1 pinch sage, for each veal	1 tablespoon parsley
8 slices of Prosciutto ham	Salt and pepper to taste
1/4 cup white wine	

Season veal with salt and pepper then lightly dust with flour.

Heat a saute pan with olive oil and cook veal for approximately 1 minute on each side. Remove pan from burner, add to each piece of veal, sage and Prosciutto. Pierce with a toothpick to keep Prosciutto from sliding off.

Return to burner add 1/4 cup of white wine and 1 teaspoon Marsala wine, cook until liquid is completely absorbed. Remove veal from saute pan and discard oil.

Add butter, water, and parsley to pan and stir with a tablespoon until warm, pour over veal and serve.

For garnish, you may add black olives.

Note:

For this veal dish, best results are achieved when cooked in an aluminum pan.

Saltimbocca Alla Romana has a flavor unmatched by any other veal dishes.

Scaloppine Di Vitello Piccata

Sauteed Veal in Lemon Wine Sauce

Ingredients / Serves 6

8 - 3 oz slices of veal

Flour

Olive oil

Juice of 1 lemon

1 1/2 cups white wine
(Chablis recommended)

1 tablespoon parsley, chopped

1/4 stick of butter

4 tablespoons water

Salt and pepper to taste

Season veal with salt and pepper then lightly dust with flour. Heat a saute pan with olive oil and cook veal for approximately 1 minute on each side. Add lemon juice and wine and cook until wine is completely absorbed. Remove veal from saute pan and discard oil.

Add parsley, butter and water to pan and stir with a tablespoon until warm, pour over veal and serve.

For garnish you may add lemon slices.

Note:

For this veal dish, best results are achieved when cooked in an aluminum pan.

An all time favorite veal specialty.

Involtini Di Vitello Con Asparàgi

Rolled Veal with Asparagus

Ingredients / Serves 6

24 pieces of asparagus, poached

12 - 3 oz slices of veal

1/2 pinch sage, for each slice of veal

12 slices of Prosciutto ham

12 slices of Fontina cheese, thin

Olive oil

2 cloves garlic

Flour

1/3 cup white wine (Chablis recommended)

Juice of 1 lemon

1/2 cup water

4 tablespoons butter

1 tablespoon fresh parsley, chopped

Salt and pepper to taste

To poach asparagus: boil asparagus in salt water until tender, approximately 8 minutes. Drain and set aside.

Begin by seasoning one side of veal with salt and pepper and a 1/2 pinch of sage. Place Prosciutto, Fontina cheese and 2 pieces of asparagus on top of each piece of veal. Roll and pierce with a toothpick.

Heat a saute pan with olive oil and garlic. Remove garlic when golden brown. Dust veal with flour and brown each piece of rolled veal on all sides. Add white wine, lemon juice and simmer until completely absorbed.

Place veal in a shallow baking pan and set aside. Drain excess oil from saute pan. Add water and butter and stir with a tablespoon until warm, then pour over veal, sprinkle with parsley and serve.

Note:

For this veal dish, best results are achieved when cooked in aluminum pan.

A unique blend of flavors arise from this veal specialty.

Scaloppine Di Vitello Con Funghi

Sliced Veal with Mushrooms

Ingredients / Serves 6

8 - 4 oz pieces of veal

1 lb mushrooms, sliced and poached

1/2 lemon

3/4 cup white wine (Chablis recommended)

Olive oil

2 cloves garlic

Flour

1 tablespoon parsley

1 tablespoon fresh basil

1/4 cup water

Salt and pepper to taste

To poach mushrooms: boil water with 1/2 lemon, salt, and 1/4 cup of white wine. Add mushrooms and boil until water boils again. Drain, pat dry and set aside.

In saute pan heat olive oil and garlic. Remove garlic when golden brown. Season veal with salt and pepper and dust with flour. Saute veal for approximately 1 minute on each side. Then add parsley, basil, mushrooms and 1/2 cup white wine.

When wine is absorbed the veal is done. Place veal on a serving dish and discard oil from pan. Add a 1/4 cup water to pan, mix then serve on top of veal.

Note:

For this veal dish, best results are achieved when cooked in an aluminum pan.

A light and flavorful veal entree.

Scaloppine Di Vitello Al Marsala

Sliced Veal with Marsala Wine

Ingredients / Serves 4

8 - 4 oz slices of veal	3 tablespoons unsalted butter
Flour	1/4 cup water
Olive oil	Salt and pepper to taste
1/2 cup dry Marsala wine	

Season veal with salt and pepper then lightly dust with flour. Heat a saute pan with olive oil and cook veal for 1 minute on each side. Add Marsala wine and cook until wine is completely absorbed.

Remove veal and set aside. Discard oil from pan. Add butter and water to pan and stir with a tablespoon until warm, pour over veal and serve.

Note:

Suggested Dry Marsala - "Florio" Brand.

Note:

For this veal dish, best results are achieved when cooked in an aluminum pan.

A classic Veal Marsala with Aldo's special touch.

Rognóncino Di Vitello Alla Paesana

Veal Kidney Country Style

Ingredients / Serves 4

2 veal kidney

1/2 cup wine vinegar

4 cups water

Olive oil

1 Spanish onion, sliced

4 pear tomatoes, peeled, seeded and chopped

1 pinch parsley

1 pinch oregano

2 pinches basil

Salt and pepper to taste

Begin by trimming fat from veal kidney. Next slice kidney thin and place in bowl with wine vinegar and water. Keep immersed until kidney becomes white in color. Remove and rinse with cold water. Set aside.

Coat a large saute pan with olive oil and add sliced onion, veal kidney, tomato, parsley, oregano, basil, salt and pepper to taste. Place saute pan over high heat. Cook until done.

Classic elegance to veal kidneys.

Fegato Di Vitello Alla Aldo

Calf Liver Aldo Style

Ingredients / Serves 4

8 slices of calves liver

Olive Oil

1 Spanish onion, sliced

4 tomatoes, peeled and seeded

1 pinch sage

1 teaspoon parsley

Flour

Salt and pepper to taste

Coat a large saute pan with olive oil, add sliced onion and cook until tender. Next add tomatoes, sage, and parsley. Cook until warm. Dust calf liver with flour on both sides, place in saute pan, add salt and pepper to taste. Cook 5 minutes on each side until tender. Place on platter and serve.

Calve's liver never tasted better when prepared in this fashion.

Pollo

Spezzato Di Pollo Alla Cacciatora

Chicken in a Light Tomato Sauce

Ingredients / Serves 6

1 1/2 lbs mushrooms, sliced and poached

Juice from 1/2 lemon

1 1/4 cups white wine (Chablis recommended)

1 cup olive oil

8 cloves garlic

3 - 2 lb spring chickens, cut in eight pieces (separate legs, wings, split breast & thigh, lightly flour)

1 Spanish onion, julienne

3 pinches rosemary leaves

6 pear tomatoes, peeled, seeded, and chopped lightly

4 cups chicken broth

2 tablespoon parsley, chopped

Salt and Pepper to taste

To poach mushrooms, boil water with juice of 1/2 lemon, and 1/4 cup of white wine. Add mushrooms and boil for 8 minutes. Drain and set aside.

In a saute pan heat olive oil, and garlic. Remove garlic when golden brown. Add chicken and season with salt and pepper. Cook approximately 10 minutes, add mushrooms, onions and saute over medium heat until onions are tender. Add 1 cup white wine and rosemary and cook until wine is completely absorbed.

Return to heat. Add tomatoes, chicken broth, parsley, salt and pepper to taste. Continue cooking until chicken and sauce are reduced, approximately 20 to 35 minutes and serve.

Chef Aldo's own touch for this traditional chicken dish.

Petti Di Pollo Alla Piemontese

Chicken with Peppers and White Wine

Ingredients / Serves 6

2 red bell peppers	1 pinch rosemary
2 yellow peppers	1 teaspoon anchovy paste
Olive oil	2 tablespoons parsley, chopped
4 cloves garlic	1 pinch crushed red pepper
12 boneless chicken breasts	1 cup water
Flour	1/4 stick unsalted butter
1/4 cup white wine (Chablis recommended)	Salt and Pepper to taste

Preheat oven to 450° F.

Roast peppers in a large shallow baking pan until skin is blanched. Remove peppers from pan and place in cold water to remove skin. Slice pepper into 1/2" strips. Set aside.

Heat a saute pan with olive oil and garlic. Remove garlic when golden brown. Salt and pepper chicken breast and lightly dust with flour. Add chicken to saute pan, cook approximately 2 minutes each side. Add wine and cook until wine is completely absorbed. Remove chicken and set aside.

In the same saute pan over low heat, add rosemary, anchovy paste, roasted peppers, parsley, crushed red pepper, water and butter. Return chicken to pan, stir and cook approximately 4 minutes or until sauce is reduced to desired consistency. Place chicken and sauce in a large shallow baking pan. Cook in oven until chicken is tender. Arrange on serving plate and serve.

Northern Italian style, light and nutritous.

Petti Di Pollo Ripieni Alla Aldo

Chicken Stuffed with Ham and Cheese

Ingredients / Serves 6

6 - 5 oz boneless chicken breasts, butterfly cut

2 tablespoons parsley, chopped

1 teaspoon sage

3 slices of white bread, crust removed, diced fine

6 slices Prosciutto ham, diced fine

12 slices Swiss cheese, 6 diced fine, 6 whole slices

2 egg yolks

Olive oil

4 cloves garlic

Flour

1/2 cup white wine (Chablis recommended)

12 mushroom caps, par boiled

1/4 stick butter

1/2 cup heavy whipping cream, warm

Salt and pepper to taste

Preheat oven to 350° F.

Butterfly each chicken breast and pound slightly. Season both sides with salt and pepper.

In a mixing bowl combine 1 tablespoon parsley, 1/2 teaspoon sage, white of bread, Prosciutto and diced cheese. Add egg yolks and mix until bread is moistened. Add stuffing to chicken breast, roll and fasten with toothpicks.

Heat a saute pan with olive oil and garlic. Remove garlic when golden brown. Dust chicken with flour and brown each piece two minutes on each side.

Add wine, salt and pepper, and cook until wine is absorbed. Place in a large shallow baking pan. Cover each with 1 slice of Swiss cheese and 2 mushroom caps. Bake for approximately 25 minutes.

Remove and place on serving dish.

For sauce: Discard oil from pan, add butter and melt. Add warm cream, mix thoroughly and spoon over chicken.

Chicken with a light and flavorful stuffing.

Petti Di Pollo Con Verdure Alla Toscana

Sauteed Chicken with White Wine and Vegetables

Ingredients / Serves 6

12 - 3 oz boneless chicken breasts

6 oz olive oil

4 cloves garlic, whole

Flour

3 stalks celery, diced

2 carrots, cut round

1 medium Spanish onion, julienne

1 tablespoon parsley

1 pinch sage

1 pinch rosemary

1/4 cup water

1/2 cup dry white wine

4 pear tomatoes, seeded and chopped

1 tablespoon parsley

Salt and pepper to taste

Preheat oven to 450° F.

Heat a saute pan with olive oil and garlic. Remove garlic when golden brown. Dust chicken with flour, brown both sides of each piece.

Add celery, carrots, onions, parsley, sage, rosemary and 1/4 cup water. Cook until vegetables are tender. Add wine and cook until wine is completely absorbed. Add tomatoes, parsley, salt and pepper to taste.

Bake until chicken is tender. Remove chicken and place on a serving platter.

This is one of Chef Aldo's favorites.

Spezzato Di Pollo Con Carciofini

Chicken with Baby Artichokes

Ingredients / Serves 6

2 spring chickens about 2 1/2 lbs each, split in half and cleaned thoroughly

12 baby artichokes, cut in half

Olive oil

6 cloves garlic

Flour

1 pinch fresh mint, chopped

1 cup white wine (Chablis recommended)

1 tablespoon parsley, chopped

Salt and pepper to taste

Preheat oven to 400° F.

Clean artichokes and par-boil in water until tender. Strain and set aside.

Coat large shallow baking pan with olive oil. On stove, heat olive oil and add garlic. Remove garlic when golden brown. Lightly dust chicken with flour, place in baking pan. Add mint, salt and pepper to taste. Bake for 25 to 30 minutes. Add wine, artichokes and parsley. Continue baking in preheated oven until chicken is tender, approximately 10-15 minutes and serve.

Note:

To preserve color of artichokes, 1) place lemon in cold water before boiling. 2) dissolve 1 tablespoon of flour with 1/4 cup of wine and add to boiling water.

A colorful and tasty chicken entree.

Pesce

Involtini Di Salmone Orto Mare

Filet of Salmon

Ingredients / Serves 6

6 - 6 oz slices of salmon, butterfly cut

5 oz bag spinach

1/3 cup Parmesan cheese, grated

8 tablespoons ricotta cheese

2 egg yolks

Flour

2 tablespoons olive oil

2 cloves garlic

1/2 leek, sliced

1 pinch parsley

Salt and pepper to taste

Sauce:

1/2 cup white wine

1 pinch dry mustard

1/4 cup whipping cream

Begin by butterflying salmon and season with salt and pepper.

In a bowl add cooked and strained chopped spinach, Parmesan cheese, ricotta cheese, egg yolks and salt and pepper to taste. Mix thoroughly, place mixture into salmon and roll.

Dust salmon with flour and salt and pepper to taste. In a large saute pan heat olive oil with garlic. Remove garlic when golden brown. Add sliced leeks and parsley and cook salmon on each side.

Remove salmon from pan, combine white wine with dry mustard and add to saute pan, let absorb. Last add whipping cream stir and cook until done. Pour sauce over salmon and serve.

Salmon with a subtle hint of flavors from the spinach and ricotta.

Baccala Fresco Alla Aldo

Cod Fish Aldo style

Ingredients / Serves 6

6 - 8 oz fresh filets of cod
Olive oil

1 Spanish onion, julienne

12 fresh Roma tomatoes,
peeled, seeded and julienne

1 tablespoon fresh parsley,
chopped

1 cup white raisins

1/2 cup pine nuts

Salt and pepper to taste

Heat a saute pan with olive oil and add onions, cook until tender. Add tomatoes, parsley, raisins and pine nuts. Continue cooking until tomatoes are tender. In same saute pan cook fish until golden brown. Remove fish and pour sauce mixture over top and serve.

Light, flaky and accented by the fresh tomatoes.

Bistecca Di Tonno Al Forno Alla Erbe

Tuna with Fresh Herbs

Ingredients / Serves 6

6 - 6 oz tuna steaks, 1/2 inch thick

Extra virgin olive oil

Flour

1/2 cup white wine

1 teaspoon anchovy paste

1/2 tablespoon fresh tarragon

1 pinch fresh rosemary

Juice of 1 lemon

1 tablespoon capers, chopped

2 tablespoons fresh parsley, chopped

Salt and pepper to taste

Preheat oven to 400° F.

Coat a large shallow baking pan with olive oil. Lightly dust tuna filets with flour and place in pan. Salt and pepper to taste.

In a mixing bowl combine wine, anchovy paste, tarragon, rosemary, lemon juice and chopped capers. Mix thoroughly and pour mixture over filets and bake approximately 20 minutes. Sprinkle with chopped parsley and serve.

Note:

Do not overcook as tuna may become too dry.

Fresh herbs will make this a memorable dish.

Pesce Spada Alla Aldo

Swordfish with Sweet Red Onions

Ingredients / Serves 6

6 - 6 oz swordfish steaks, 1/2 inch thick

Olive oil

Flour

1 tablespoon parsley

1 teaspoon oregano

1 teaspoon basil

6 Roma tomatoes, peeled, seeded and chopped

1 sweet red onion, sliced

1/4 cup white wine

Salt and pepper to taste

Preheat oven to 400° F.

Coat a large shallow baking pan with olive oil. Lightly dust swordfish with flour and place in pan. Sprinkle with parsley, oregano, basil, tomato, onion and wine. Bake approximately 25 minutes and serve.

The texture of the Swordfish when prepared this way in quite unique.

Orange Roughy

Ingredients / Serves 6

6 - 6 oz Orange Roughy filets

1 tablespoon Dijon mustard

1/2 cup white wine (Chablis recommended)

1 tablespoon parsley

1 pinch rosemary

1 pinch thyme

6 green olives, chopped

Juice of 1/2 lemon

Olive oil

4 cloves garlic, sliced

Salt and pepper to taste

Preheat oven to 400° F.

In a mixing bowl combine mustard, wine, parsley, rosemary, thyme, olives and lemon juice. Mix thoroughly and set aside.

Coat large shallow baking pan with olive oil. Place filets in pan, salt and pepper to taste. Add garlic on top of filets and pour sauce over. Bake until tender. Serve with lemon wedge.

Aldo's Italian accent to this Orange Roughy recipe.

Trota Di Lago Al' Aneto

Lake Trout with Dill

Ingredients / Serves 6

6 - 6 oz lake trout
Olive oil
1 teaspoon mustard
1/4 cup white wine
1 pinch paprika

1 tablespoon fresh dill, chopped
1 pinch parsley
Salt and pepper to taste

Brush lake trout with olive oil, mustard, and white wine. Coat saute pan with olive oil and add fish. Sprinkle lake trout with paprika, dill, parsley, salt and pepper to taste. Cook both sides until golden brown. Serve with lemon wedge.

Simple to prepare, and subtle in taste.

Trancia Di Salmone Al Forno

Salmon Steak With Wild Oyster Mushrooms

Ingredients / Serves 6

6 salmon steaks

1 lb Oyster mushrooms, poached

Juice of 1/2 lemon

3/4 cup white wine

Olive oil

Flour

1 leek sliced

1 tablespoon fresh basil

1/3 cup whipping cream

1 tablespoon unsalted butter

Parsley

Salt and pepper to taste

Preheat oven to 400° F.

To poach mushrooms, boil water with juice of 1/2 lemon, salt and 1/4 cup of white wine. Add mushrooms and boil for 8 minutes. Drain and set aside.

Coat large shallow baking pan with olive oil. Place flour dusted salmon in pan, season both sides with salt and pepper. Cover salmon with remaining 1/2 cup of wine, sliced leek, poached mushrooms and basil. Bake until salmon is tender and flaky.

Remove salmon from pan. Add whipping cream, butter and parsley. Mix thoroughly with a tablespoon. Re-heat then pour sauce over salmon and serve.

This palate pleaser is one of Aldo's favorite fish selections.

Pecse Persico

Fried Fresh Lake Perch

Ingredients / Serves 6

6 - 6 oz portions of fresh Michigan lake perch

2 cups flour

Salt and pepper to taste

Olive Oil

For Tartar Sauce:

1 1/2 cup mayonnaise

2 hard boiled eggs, chopped

6 green olives, chopped

1 dill pickle, chopped

3 peperoncini, chopped - remove seeds

1 teaspoon Dijon mustard

1 teaspoon parsley

For tartar sauce: Mix mayonnaise, eggs, olives, pickle, peperoncini, mustard and parsley. Chill.

Combine flour, salt and pepper. In a saute pan heat olive oil. Lightly dust filets with flour mixture. Place in pan and cook approximately 4 minutes each side or until golden brown.

Serve with chilled tartar sauce and lemon wedges.

Aldo's recipe for perch Italian style.

Code Di Aragosta Alla Aldo

Lobster Tails Aldo Style

Ingredients / Serves 6

12 - 8 oz lobster tails

2 tablespoons vinegar

1 onion, chopped

2 stalks celery, chopped

1 carrot, chopped

Parsley

Dijon mustard

Lemon juice

1 stick butter

12 slices Swiss cheese

Paprika

Salt and pepper to taste

Bechamel Sauce:

1/4 stick butter

1/4 cup flour

1 1/2 cup milk, warm

1 pinch salt

1 pinch nutmeg

Preheat oven to 400° F.

Place lobster in a large pot of cold water. Add vinegar, onion, celery, carrots and parsley. Bring to a boil and continue for eight minutes. Remove lobster, rinse with cold water and set aside.

For Bechamel Sauce:

In a saute pan melt 1/4 cup butter, remove from burner and add 1/4 cup of flour stirring thoroughly with a tablespoon. In a separate saute pan, warm milk. Slowly add the milk to flour and butter mixture and add 1 pinch salt and nutmeg. Cook on low heat to desired consistency. If too thick add more milk.

Partially loosen lobster meat from shell, and spread a small amount of Dijon mustard between lobster and shell. Place lobster in a large shallow baking pan. Sprinkle each tail with lemon juice, melted butter, salt and pepper.

Pour small amount of bechamel sauce on tails, cover with Swiss cheese and sprinkle with paprika. Bake in oven until cheese melts and serve with drawn butter.

Lobster tails never tasted this good.

70

Agnello & Maiale

Bistcchine Di Agnello Alla Aldo

Lamb Chops Sauteed Alla Aldo

Ingredients / Serves 4

12 rib lamb chops	6 cloves garlic, sliced
Olive oil	1 tablespoon red wine vinegar
Flour	1 teaspoon water
1 pinch rosemary	Salt and pepper to taste

Preheat oven to 400° F.

Heat a large saute pan with olive oil. Trim excess fat from lamb chops, lightly dust with flour and place in saute pan. Add salt and pepper to taste, rosemary, garlic. Cook lamb chops 2 minutes on each side then add red wine vinegar, water and cook until absorbed. Place in oven and bake for five minutes and serve.

Sweet and delicious.

Spezzato Di Angello Con Piselli Alla Aldo

Lamb Stew with Peas Alla Aldo

Ingredients / Serves 6

3 pounds boneless lamb shoulder in 3/4 inch cubes

Olive oil

1/4 stick butter

2 cloves garlic, quartered

3 pinches rosemary

1 tablespoon parsley

1 pinch hot red pepper seeds

2 Knob onions, sliced

1/3 cup Burgundy wine

Handful of flour

2 cups water

1 tablespoon tomato paste

1 1/2 cups par boiled peas

Salt and pepper to taste

Heat a large sauce pan with olive oil, butter and garlic. Remove garlic when golden brown. Add meat and brown on all sides. Add rosemary, parsley, hot red pepper seeds, sliced onions, salt and pepper to taste. Cook approximately 2 minutes. Add Burgundy wine and let simmer until wine is absorbed. Remove from burner and sprinkle with flour, stir thoroughly. Add water and tomato paste. Cook on low heat for 20 to 25 minutes. Add peas, mix thoroughly and serve.

Note:

If stew is too thick add water.

The blending of the vegetables and seasonings make this dish stand out.

Coscio Di Agnello Arrosto

Roasted Leg of Lamb

Ingredients / Serves 6

1 boneless leg of lamb, about 4 lbs

1 pinch rosemary

6 cloves garlic, sliced

Flour

Olive Oil

For Sauce:

2 celery stalks, chopped

2 carrots, chopped

1 large onion, sliced

1 pinch parsley

2 Pear tomatoes, peeled and seeded

2 bay leaves

1 cup white wine

3 cups water

1/2 cup flour

Salt and pepper to taste

Preheat oven to 400° F.

Season lamb inside and outside with rosemary, garlic, salt and pepper. Sprinkle with flour. Tie lamb in a cross pattern with butchers string. Coat roasting pan with olive oil. Place lamb in pan. Bake for 30 minutes.

Lower oven temperature to 350° F. Add celery, carrots, onion, parsley, tomatoes, bay leaves, white wine and water. Continue baking for 45 minutes. Remove lamb from oven. Skim excess oil. Add 1/2 cup flour, stir thoroughly. Slice lamb and place on a serving platter, strain sauce then pour sauce over top and serve.

Aldo's version of leg of lamb is one to be remembered.

Bistecchine Di Maiale Alla Aldo

Pork Chops Alla Aldo

Ingredients / Serves 4

8 loin pork chops 1/2" thick with bone in

Olive oil

4 cloves garlic, mashed

Flour

2 pinches fennel seeds

2 bay leafs, whole

1/4 cup Chablis wine

16 Greek olives

Salt and pepper to taste

Preheat oven to 400° F. Coat a large shallow baking pan with olive oil. Add garlic, heat on stove top and remove garlic when golden brown. Lightly dust pork chops with flour and add to pan.

Saute on high heat until browned on both sides. Sprinkle with fennel seeds, add bay leaves, salt and pepper to taste, wine and Greek olives. Cook until wine is absorbed, then finish cooking in oven until desired temperature is achieved. Discard excess oil. Place pork chops on a serving platter and serve with 4 olives each.

Pork chops both juicy and flavorful.

Fettine Di Maiale Alla Salvia E Vino Bianco

Sliced Pork Loin with Sage and White Wine

Ingredients / Serves 6

12 - 3 oz pork loin, sliced thin

Olive oil

4 cloves garlic

Flour

2 pinches sage

2 pinches parsley

1 1/2 cup white wine

Salt and pepper to taste

In a large saute pan add olive oil and garlic cloves. Remove garlic when golden brown. Dust pork with flour and add to hot saute pan, cook for 2 minutes on both sides then add sage, parsley and white wine. Let wine absorb until pork starts to stick to pan. Remove pork, and place on a serving dish. Remove oil from pan and add a little water, stir with wooden tablespoon then pour over pork.

Elegance and simplicity are characteristics of this pork dish.

Risòtto & Vegetali

Risotto Rustico Con Carciofini E Piselli Alla Aldo

Rice with Baby Artichokes and Peas

Ingredients / Serves 6

2 cups peas	1/4 cup white wine
12 baby artichokes, quartered	2 tablespoons parsley
Juice of 1/2 lemon	1 pinch mint
Olive Oil	1 tablespoon tomato paste, for color
1/4 stick butter	
2 cloves garlic, mashed	12 cups water, boiled
12 green onions, white part only	Salt and pepper to taste
	2 tablespoons Parmesan cheese
1/8 lb prosciutto ham, julienne	
3 cups rice	2 tablespoon Romano cheese

Parboil peas in cold salted water. Strain and set aside.

Par boil artichokes in salted water with juice of 1/2 lemon. Strain and set aside.

Coat a 12" baking pan with olive oil. Add butter, garlic, sliced green onions and prosciutto.

Cook 5-7 minutes on stove top over medium heat and add raw rice and wine.

Mix thoroughly with a tablespoon until wine absorbs. Add parsley, mint and tomato paste. Continue mixing thoroughly.

Slowly add boiled water, a small amount at a time enough to cover rice. Let simmer until water is absorbed. Continue adding water, repeat simmer and absorb.

Add cooked artichokes, peas, salt and pepper to taste.

Continue to simmer until rice is done to al-dente. Sprinkle with Parmesan and Romano cheese and serve.

A classic country–style rice entree.

Risotto Misto Di Pesce Alla Aldo

Rice with Mixed Fish

Ingredients / Serves 6

12 cups water

Olive oil

1/4 stick butter

3 cloves garlic, mashed

6 calamari, cleaned and sliced

1 onion, diced fine

3 cups rice

1/4 cup white wine

1 tablespoon tomato paste

12 shrimp, cut in pieces

2 lobster tails, cleaned and cut in pieces

Black pepper

Salt to taste

2 pinches basil

1 pinch hot pepper seeds

2 tablespoons parsley

Juice of 1/4 lemon

In a large pot boil 12 cups salted water.

Coat a 12" shallow baking pan with olive oil. Add butter, mashed garlic, raw calamari and diced onion. Cook 5-7 minutes on stove top over high heat.

Add rice and mix together. Add white wine. Let wine absorb into rice, then add boiling salted water, enough to cover rice, cook until water is absorbed. Add additional boiling water to cover rice again, add tomato paste and mix together. Add cut shrimp, lobster and black pepper, salt, basil, hot pepper seeds, parsley and lemon juice. Cook until rice is done. You may adjust spices to your taste.

Parmesan cheese is optional.

This seafood rendition is both appetizing and nutritional.

Risotto Con Brodo Di Pollo E Funghi Porcini Alla Aldo

Rice with Chicken Broth and Dry Porcini Mushrooms

Ingredients / Serves 6

18 cups chicken broth

2 cups dry Porcini mushrooms

12 cups water

Olive oil

1/4 stick butter

1 onion, diced

1 pinch saffron

1 pinch parsley

2 pinches basil

1 pinch mint

1 tablespoon salt

2 pinches pepper

3 cups rice

1/4 cup white wine

2 tablespoons Parmesan cheese

In a pot over low heat begin by heating chicken broth to a boil.

In a pot of hot water soak Porcini mushrooms until soft. Set aside.

Coat a 12" shallow baking pan with olive oil. Add butter, and onions. Cook on stove top over high heat until onions are tender.

Remove mushrooms from water. Save the water, strain thoroughly.

Add mushrooms to baking pan.

Add saffron, parsley, basil, mint, 1 tablespoon salt, and 2 pinches of pepper. Let simmer for 5 to 7 minutes.

Add raw rice and wine. Mix thoroughly with a tablespoon until wine is absorbed.

Slowly add chicken broth and the strained water from the mushrooms, a small amount at a time enough to cover rice. Let simmer until water is absorbed. Continue adding broth and water, repeat simmer and absorb. Continue cooking until rice is tender to al-dente. Top with Parmesan cheese and serve.

The Porcini mushrooms give this dish its distinctive flavor.

Cavolfióre Gratinato Al Forno

Baked Cauliflower Au Gratin

Ingredients / Serves 6

2 small heads cauliflower	Bechamel Sauce:
1 lemon wedge	4 tablespoons butter
6 oz Fontina cheese, grated	4 tablespoons flour
1/2 cup Parmesan cheese	3 cups milk
Dash Paprika	1 dash nutmeg
1 pinch parsley	Salt and Pepper to taste

Preheat oven to 350° F.

Clean cauliflower thoroughly, break into flowerettes, boil in salted water with lemon wedge until tender. Drain and set aside.

For Bechamel Sauce:

Melt butter in sauce pan. Add flour to butter, cook approximately 1/2 minute. Add warm milk, nutmeg, salt and pepper to taste. Stir until Bechamel becomes thick.

Place cauliflower in baking pan, cover with bechamel sauce. Sprinkle with Fontina cheese, Parmesan, paprika, and parsley. Cover with aluminum foil, and bake until cheese is melted and serve.

This tasty cauliflower dish will accompany any entree.

Piselli Con Prosciutto E Cipolline

Peas with Prosciutto and Green Onions

Ingredients / Serves 6

2 tablespoons butter

3 green onions, sliced

6 slices Prosciutto ham, julienne

3 cups sweet peas

1/4 cup chicken broth

Flour

Salt and pepper to taste

Melt butter in saute pan. Add green onions and Prosciutto. Cook until Prosciutto is slightly crispy. Add peas and broth, sprinkle with flour. Add salt and pepper to taste. Cook until peas are tender and serve.

The blending of the Prosciutto brings on added flavor to this dish.

Broccolo

Boiled Broccoli

Ingredients / Serves 6

3 bunches broccoli
1/2 cup olive oil
2 cloves garlic, sliced
Salt and pepper to taste

Remove skins from stalks and wash broccoli thoroughly. Cook in boiling water with a pinch of salt until tender. Strain broccoli and place on a serving dish. Sprinkle with olive oil, sliced garlic, salt and pepper to taste. Serve at room temperature.

Healthy, tasty and low in fat.

Eggplant Alla Parmigiana

Baked Eggplant with Tomato Sauce and Parmesan Cheese

Ingredients / Serves 6

2 medium eggplants

Olive oil

1 Spanish onion, julienne

32 oz tomatoes, chopped

1 pinch basil

1 pinch oregano

1 tablespoon parsley

1/2 cup water

18 slices mozzarella cheese

1/2 cup Parmesan cheese, grated

Salt and pepper to taste

Preheat oven to 350° F.

Cut eggplant lengthwise 1/2 inch thick. Sprinkle with salt and place on a strainer. Set aside for 40 minutes.

For sauce, coat sauce pan with olive oil, add onions and cook until tender. Add tomatoes, basil, oregano, parsley and 1/2 cup of water. Cook thoroughly.

Take eggplant, wash off salt in cold water then dry with paper towel and brush with olive oil and grill each side until tender.

In a small baking pan, place a layer of egg plant, cover with sauce, sprinkle with Parmesan cheese then add a layer of mozzarella cheese. Repeat this process until all ingredients are used. Cover with aluminum foil and bake 25 minutes until cheese is melted and serve.

This dish could double as an entree.

Patate Al Pomodoro Alla Aldo

Potatoes with Tomatoes

Ingredients / Serves 4

4 medium Idaho potatoes	1 teaspoon basil
Olive oil	1/2 teaspoon oregano
1 Spanish onion, sliced	1 tablespoon parsley
4 pear tomatoes, chopped, peeled and seeded	Salt and pepper to taste

To proceed, boil potatoes with skin on, keep firm. Drain and remove skins when potatoes reach room temperature. When cool slice potatoes in 1/4" pieces. Place on side.

In a large saute pan, coat with olive oil and add sliced onion. Cook until onions are tender. Add chopped tomato and mix thoroughly. Next add basil, oregano, potatoes, parsley, salt and pepper to taste. Heat over medium heat for 15 to 20 minutes. Serve hot.

A vegetable accompaniment that will go with any entree.

Patate Arrostite Al Forno

Roasted Potato with Garlic and Rosemary

Ingredients / Serves 6

4 medium Idaho potatoes

1 tablespoon butter

3 cloves garlic

2 pinches rosemary

Olive oil, sufficient to coat bottom of pan

Salt and pepper to taste

Preheat oven to 350° F.

Peel potatoes, cut into quarters. Place in shallow baking pan. Add butter, garlic, rosemary, olive oil, salt and pepper to taste. Mix thoroughly, place in oven, bake until golden brown and tender.

Hearty, but not too filling.

Patate Alla Crema

Potatoes with Cream

Ingredients / Serves 4

4 medium Idaho potatoes	Parsley
Milk, sufficient to cover potatoes	2 tablespoons Parmesan cheese
1 stick butter	Salt and pepper to taste

Preheat oven to 350° F.

Slice potatoes into thin pieces. Place in shallow baking pan add salt and pepper to taste. Cover potatoes half way with milk and butter, sprinkle parsley and Parmesan cheese over the entire mixture. Cover with aluminum foil and bake until tender. Uncover and continue cooking for 10 additional minutes for color.

A potato dish that goes well with pork and fish.

Dolce

Tiramisu

Ingredients / Serves 6

4 eggs separated (save all yolks - save only 1 white)

1/2 cup sugar

1 lb Mascarpone cheese

2 oz unsweetened chocolate, grated

2 cups chilled espresso coffee

1/8 cup rum

1 package lady fingers

Powdered cocoa

Mix egg yolks and sugar until sugar is almost dissolved. Next add Mascarpone cheese and whip together. Beat egg white in a separate bowl until thick, then fold gently into cheese mixture. Add grated chocolate. Mix espresso and rum together in a separate bowl.

Dip lady fingers lightly in coffee and rum mixture and line the bottom of the pan. Add 1/2 of the cream mixture. Line the rest of the pan with lady fingers going in the opposite direction of bottom layer. Top with remaining cream mixture. Sprinkle top with cocoa, chill before serving.

Aldo's deliciously decadent ending to a perfect meal.

Zabaione Freddo Per Frutta Di Stagione

Cold Zabaione with Fresh Fruit in Season

Ingredients / Serves 4

4 egg yolks

5 tablespoons sugar

4 tablespoons dry Marsala wine

1 pint whipping cream

First make Zabaione: in a small double boiler add egg yolks, wine and 4 tablespoons of sugar. Whisk over medium heat until thick and smooth. Then remove from heat. To cool take another bowl, fill with ice then take bowl with mixture and lay on top of ice.

Add whipping cream in a separate bowl that is chilled then whip until thick. Add 1 spoon of sugar and continue until thick.

Gently fold the whipping cream into the Zabaione. Chill until ready to serve.

After Zabaione has chilled you can serve by topping it with fresh fruit of the season.

Cool, light and delicious, especially over fresh berries.

Custard Pasticceria

Pastry custard

Ingredients / Serves 6

6 egg yolks	3 cups milk
6 tablespoons sugar	3 lemon peels chopped fine
6 tablespoons flour	1/2 teaspoon butter

In a mixing bowl, mix egg yolks and sugar. After egg yolks and sugar are thoroughly mixed, slowly stir in flour. Set the mixture aside.

In a saute pan add 3 cups milk, 3 lemon peels, and heat to luke warm. Next add milk to sugar, egg and flour mixture. Place in a double boiler and bring to a boil. When done add butter to cream mixture and stir with a whisk.

This sumptuous dessert has the subtle taste of lemon.

Zuppa Inglese Crema Pasticceria

Ingredients / Serves 6

6 egg yolks

6 tablespoons sugar

6 tablespoons flour

6 1/3 oz. milk

2 lemon peels

1 teaspoon sugar

1 teaspoon butter

3 package 14 oz. Vicenzi Saviardo Biscuits

Cream D'Almond liquor

Whipping cream

For custard:

In a sauce pan add egg yolks and 6 tablespoons sugar. Mix thoroughly. Next add flour and continue mixing. In a separate pan bring milk to a warm temperature then add to original mixture. Place ingredients and lemon peel into a double boiler and cook until mixture thickens. Add butter and stir briefly.

In a 12 inch square baking pan place one layer of biscuits over entire surface. Sprinkle lightly with almond liquor and cover with custard. Repeat the process to desired number of layers, possibly 3 to 4.

After complete, top with whipping cream. Keep refrigerated until ready to serve.

Note:

1 bean of vanilla is optional for custard.

The Vicenzi Saviardo Biscuits are a must in this recipe.